The Call Of a

SHEPHERD'S

Song

By Michael Doyle

"With all my love, I dedicate this book to my beloved daughters, Angelique and Sierra. You are the melody in my soul and the light in my days. Your faith, strength, and kindness inspire me beyond measure. May you always walk in truth and love, and know that you are cherished more than words can say...."

Table of Contents

Tale of Christmas in Two Parts

by Michael Doyle

I.

I have heard it said
That you can eat 'til you're full
And it's still not enough
The excuse to be given
"But, it's Christmas…"
And one really shouldn't miss this
More cake to take
For Heaven's sake
And in the spirit of….
Well gluttony, I'll have some more

I have heard it said
That you can have all you need
And it's still not enough
The excuse to be given
"But, it's Christmas…"
And one really should not do without
More bells and whistles
Gizmos and gears
And in the spirit of…
Well, envy, I'll take some more

I have heard it said
One can never have enough lovers
No penitent of desire
There is never enough
The excuse to be given
"But, it's Christmas…"
And my wants are felt like fire
To do without would be dire
And in the spirit of ….
Well, lust, I need so much more

I have heard it said
I must have all life must give me
And keep it all to myself
There is never enough
The excuse to be given
"But, it's Christmas…"
Material things are everything
So I gather these around me
And in the spirit of…
Well, greed, I will keep these things

I have heard it said
There is enough to keep me angry
And entitled I will remain so
Uncontrolled and unforgiving
The excuse to be given
"But it's Christmas is enough to suffice
I have earned this anger
It's a welcome stranger
And in the spirit of …
Well, wrath, I will give it toward others….

I have heard it said
It's too hard to do right
And easier to do nothing at all
I am sure I am forgiven
The excuse to be given
"But, it's Christmas …"
There is time enough to find God
And He should find me…
And in the spirit of …
Well, sloth, I will rely on unearned grace

….

No wait a minute
In the spirit of Christmas
I will live each day with love
Giving toward all the others
My sisters and my brothers
Each day a treasure
To be held without measure
Bringing such peace as I can

Walking life like a prayer
And filling needs where I dare

4

II.

It is said, I have heard
And yes, I believe
That absent temperance
No other virtue can be sustained
Yes, it's Christmas
And while there is time and place
For everything noble and good
It's best to control excess
And in the spirit of...
Temperance, I will do just that

It is said, and I have experienced
That is it better to give than receive
The milk of kindness nourishes both
And brings contentment
Yes, it's Christmas
The study of kindness
Is the essence of love
Without which we are undone
So, in the spirit of...
Kindness, I will share just that

I have heard it said and have come to know
The best path to true love is purity
A cardinal rule for holy living
Is that each phase of love has time and place
Yes, it is Christmas
The sexual union remaining best in marriage
And we've all seen the harm done
When we've not followed this one
So, in the spirit of....
Chastity, I will practice just that

I have heard it said, and believe
That man's unity and friendship with God
Is kept through the habit of charity
Perfecting our spirit is in giving
Yes, it is Christmas
Glorifying the reflective nature of God
Love of God, love of man
Without which I am nothing
Charity, I will share this love

I have heard it said
And I believe persistence and endurance
Without anger and in forbearance
It provides the strength so needed
Yes, it is Christmas
And as the fruit of the Holy Spirit
Let us practice this with each other
With all our sisters and our brothers
So, in the spirit of...
Patience, I will offer up mine

I have heard it said and believe
All of these things must be kept
In steadfast application
As a devoted discipline
Yes, it is Christmas
I will strive to increase my qualities
To keep each of the above as part of me
In reliance, I will keep my faith
So, in the spirit of …
Diligence, I will work to perfect my soul

....

Yes, it is worth every minute
To keep the spirit of Christmas
I will live each day with love
Giving toward all the others
My sisters and my brothers
Each day, a treasure
To be held without measure
Bringing such peace as I can
Walking life like a prayer
And keeping each of these as best that I dare

Advent's Adoration

by Michael Doyle

Our eyes are open wide in adoration
Today marks the start of the Advent season
Joined hands pray for our blessing
Assured as we are without need for guessing

The pancakes made and served
Tasted better than we deserved
We find Jesus walking with us today
Immanuel came to teach us the way

In the weight of last words said
With Jesus fully aware he would soon be dead
There was a lot to know and teach
Loving one another was its total reach

Through God's eyes, His disciples walked
Listening to every word as He talked
Love was and is the sum of His theology
The cardinal virtue of His divinity

There are no strangers where love exists
Instead, there is God's joy that persists
Unafraid to follow the paths of servanthood
Kindness and love are the highest good

We show this in our lives of sacrifice
Giving our all when a little won't suffice
Daily, we take up our cross to pay the cost
The lessons in loving God will not be lost

Crucified flesh leads us to the holy ground
This is how our Lord will come to be found
No longer blinded by the temptations of the night
We faithfully follow what is known and right

It's on this path that we find our purpose
Knowing that we are born for a life of service
We are meant to live as our love overflows
With humility and uncaring of who else knows

We all know the Rebbe's story
We all fall short of our Father's glory
Yet still, we live our lives filled with love
Born to give in all ways as is Heaven above

We must surrender to God every bit of our all
Heeding as we do our Lord God's beckoning call
With arms wide open, we receive our commission
Knowing our best lives in our total submission

As we live our lives with blessed right intention
We focus our words on their correct connections
It's an amazing grace that we know abounds
It's the love of our God that freedom is truly found

One heart leads and touches another
As our lives entwine with our sisters and brothers
This is the way that love is always found there
As we reach out to God in our most solemn prayers

True faith is as contagious as a wildfire
It fills our hearts with its righteous desire
Our heavenly Father gives us His loving embrace
To pass it on within our own loving traces

Interiorly Designed

by Michael Doyle

The things that come along to discern this
That God places us where we can learn goodness
How, then, can we make the most of it and embrace
Where God has put us in our time and space

To make the most of heart, soul, and mind
To work out the best of what we might find
Most of our challenges are fought from the inside
And projected outward where these cannot hide

In the design of what makes up our minds
We find the patterns that too often bind
Are found in a world of changing conversation
We never truly bridge toward our destination

Edge to ledge forced forward to the brink
It is what we choose that brings us to think
Like Paul on a path of the untraveled road
From adversary to advocate of the Gospel, told

Damascus is calling in his prideful persecution
Until, in a pivot of grace, he is saved from destruction
In thinking, we are too often convinced that we do right
We are blinded before receiving the wisdom of light

By humility and gentleness comes the best appeal
To all that, all that is good and holy to reveal
We are best off to approach the truth with kindness
Learning to turn abrasive to persuasive in our blindness

Perhaps a little less blindness in the face-to-face
It's better to be tactful in truths we embrace
Perhaps moving past being too overly oblivious
And resolving the problems which are obvious

Though we live in this world in need of His light
We do not fight the world through the dark of night
We instead need to provide the light of love's power
To demolish the arguments captive in this hour

There is a need for gentleness, not circumspection
With a need for grace in its full contemplation
Obedient in Christ and in our every single thought
To bring about the peace needed and always sought

The resolution to problems comes in different thinking
Not in the same process of continuously linking
Where, then, are the life-stealing tensions
And how might we best these through our right intentions

Changing our thinking to change what it is we see
Our strongest thoughts give way to the possibility
What comes out in the traces of our minds
It comes out in our lives so it is that we find

What is allowed in and then allowed to root
Becomes the basis of all we ever contribute
We give power to what is most paid our attention
This is why we must wisely live with intention

As we think in our hearts, so then are we
Be careful then of what we take as authority
The Bible's lessons make the radical difference
And should be held in much accord and reverence

God's world is worn as our badges of signification
To be worn gently despite the glory's magnification
God's Word gives us the thrust of our authority
As students of this Word, we must share our legacy

Under the Potter's Hands

by Michael Doyle

Under the potter's hands
He forms the clay
We talk, He understands
We live yet another day

In our time, we fold hands
Across the world, in many lands
Talking to God quietly
Rescued from myself politely

God, in His purpose and mercy
Corrects our daily history
Amazed in the grace given
Living the love of the forgiven

We stand together, sharing our burdens
Knowing the love, however, we are hurting
Checking our hearts to ensure we're right
Marking of our own lives, the best of light

Keeping in our hearts the essence of the law
Of the Lord above as guidance for us all
These are the words that lead to wisdom
And are the keys to our Father's Kingdom

Learning to Not Be Anxious

by Michael Doyle

Tossing and turning without sleep
Filled with thoughts that won't keep
This world is filled with complexity
Enough to fill our hearts with anxiety

The restlessness of what we must endure
For all these trepidations, there is a cure
There is no failure, nor is there duplicity
But there is a need to overcome this anxiety

Rejoice then in the Lord forever and always
We must be anxious for nothing in our days
Letting God keep our minds on the good
These practical passages need to be understood

The chaos of our times raises so very high
There are enough troubles to make us cry
The reasons with certainty are solidly real
But belief and faith in God will prevail

Worrying about these things brings more harm
This is the truth: even when life loses its charm
God's pure ministry is full of truth and hope
With it, we can at last, learn how to cope

Troubles will be present but need not be a prison
These are magnified only if kept focused in a prism
It does us very little good to ruminate
Instead, meditate on the Lord and become sedated

Peter learned to walk through the storms of Galilee
Keeping his eyes focused on Jesus, his soul was free
The paper and the radio tell us to keep in fear
But hasn't God kept us safe in life, year after year?

God is the door opened by the King of all Kings
His mercy given makes him the master of all things
Bringing comfort in all causes held in despair
The bringer of comfort found in our daily prayer

Having confidence in all that, we quietly pray
Contending with whatever has passed in our day
Through the valley of the shadow of death, making our way
Rejoice in overcoming regardless of what others say

Thankful in our prayers and earnest supplication
Giving over to God all cares found in appreciation
Counting our blessings, we lift our voices in praise
Being grateful for all of our many blessed days

Don't You Just Be You

by Michael Doyle

Faith forms logic and actions
Sometimes, it's less easy with life's distractions
Doing what we really want and need
Looking at the fine print, we must read

Seek instead always to be your best
It's just reality and not a test
That loyalty to those past ways
This can sometimes lead to lesser days

Don't sacrifice your best on an altar of you
You know the right things that you must do
Taken up to the mountain for more than a view
Listen to God, He'll tell you what to do

Don't be discouraged from taking the deeper dive
Take those right decisions and be truly alive
Taking on the image in pursuing godly ways
Letting the former self pass into better days

Choosing the discomfort that serves us best
Fortified in life that we might pass this test
Striving for who we might best become
This is the way for servants of God's kingdom

Well-Tempered Clavier Played in Discord

by Michael Doyle

The disappointment
Was an assured inevitability
After all, to err is humanity's
Greatest capability

Very few are hard-wired
Into our grand design
We don't stand a prayer
In the face of the divine

Even the hand of the creator
Is open to this tragic flaw
As well intended as it is
In failing to recall

We're living wishing wishes
That seldom comes true
The best that we have
Is to hope not to rue

The shotgun wedding
That we call fate
The odds of becoming a master of puppets
Are pulled strings that come too late

The late-night shows
That used to fade into the snow
Taught us things half-forgotten
Played out in the mind's shadow

Fearing our dreams
We stay awake as long as we can
Bracing for the silent screams
From realizing we are, after all, only woman or a man

We don't have to pull the trigger
Of the metaphorical guns to our heads
Because that release is too final
We slowly filter out our perceptions instead

Like a well-tempered Clavier
Played intricately to the last note
We'd play out our parts in the passion
As if memorized by rote

On the Altar of My Life

by Michael Doyle

In every moment, even or odd
You put me together, Lord God
In every flaw and every break
You have eased every single ache

You have shown me the truth
I have lived every moment since my youth
Every shame of mine is your glory
On every turned page of your story

Somehow, you've shaped me into a man
And pushed my paths as only you can
Drawing nearer as I am to your destination
You've brought meaning to your creation

With every breath, may Christ be magnified
My enduring faith in you is signified
In my heart, I hold beauty even as I cry
I will praise you until the day that I die

You've shown me how to sacrifice
Having made an altar of my life
My heart is full of singing, and beauty in my eyes
I remain thankful for each new coming sunrise

Lifting you up with the fullness of my praise
Living your ways to my best in all of my days
On the living altar of the strains of my life
I give you the glory by every moment's sacrifice

An Appreciation Recognized

by Michael Doyle

Spoken with some adherence
Is the preacher's insistence
Only the Holy Spirit needs to appear
For the ears willing to hear

Other churches are our family
With eyes joined on the holy
We live this walk in celebration
As we spread our faith across this nation

Word and worship are our mission
The love of God is our position
As we sing ourselves a new song
With joined hands, we are where we belong

Growing faith is our witness
Our joy comes through our persistence
We follow the leadership of the Spirit
And we follow the Word as we best hear it

We are pastored in our calling
To keep us from ever falling
Growing together as one family
Let's set our eyes on all that is Holy

Thanksgiving Pause

by Michael Doyle

Fighting on until backed into the rope
We do what we can even as losing hope
I look around and see some about to shatter
It makes me wonder if our prayers matter

Some irrationally have lost the will to think
While others still lose themselves in the drink
We push from a worldly perspective's point of view
Finding instead that it just won't do

In all of our passion, we outlive those days
Putting on our best in adopting Christian ways
There's more to living in a positive light
With a Thanksgiving pause, grace sets things right

A look into a mirror shows how we finally grew
Into maturity as a new man who is new but not new
But one that has put away some childish ways
Finding genuine freedom in my born-again days

This Thanksgiving, I wonder where the year went
And what it is that accounts for all my time spent
Looking at my daughters doing schoolwork diligently
With their eyes on God, they behave so studiously

In all of our passion, we outlive those days
Putting on our best in adopting Christian ways
There's more to living in a positive light
With a Thanksgiving pause, grace sets things right

As precious as they are to me, I see their humility
No day passes that I don't see all they've taught me
Teaching lessons learned about my vast simplicity
And its value in a world overly filled with complexity

My soul is quiet and content, no longer needing more
It is as if my competing mind finally knows the score
I have seen again what it means to become as if a child
And how weaned from the world, I'm no longer defiled

In all of our passion, we outlive those days
Putting on our best in adopting Christian ways
There's more to living in a positive light
With a Thanksgiving pause, grace sets things right

My mind focuses on the Book, no longer guessing
As I watch my daughters, counting my blessings
In this life, with a heart filled with integrity
This Thanksgiving Day is spent with my family

I find my joy in the Lord and away from my old sin
Finding a cheerful heart is the best medicine
And with love such as this, I have lived the best
In God and my family, I find my heart's rest

In all of our passion, we outlive those days
Putting on our best in adopting Christian ways
There's more to living in a positive light
With a Thanksgiving pause, grace sets things right

To Make A Man Invincible

by Michael Doyle

You know that a moon full of madness
And a heart filled with sadness
Ain't never done any man no good
From that gun in your hand
It seems you just might understand
Your eyes say it is understood

Riding hard after midnight
I see your fear under the moonlight
Like you have the ghosts of your past
All the times that didn't last
Tell me now, what has you running
Is it that you're always outgunning

You; the fastest you can draw
Do you hear your fears call?
As your eyes are squinting in the sun?
How many men did you kill with that gun?
Do you hear their trembling voices?
Or were they merely choices?

There's only one thing to truly regret
That is to keep a simple secret
Out of three men, two men must be dead
That keeps stirring in the gunman's head
The silence of that which is invisible
Is the faith that makes a man feel invincible

Uncomfortable Truths Sown
by Michael Doyle

Uncomfortable truths push forward mortal history
At times, these must be sown despite the misery
and the writers of the day must dare to openly criticize
And question the prevailing order that we must analyze

However, winding or twisting the paths and trails
That gets humanity to see past our heavens and hells
It's better that we see the cruel truth past our illusion
To what we need to know and not just our comfortable delusions

In the past century, our smoke-filled eyes have learned
So many lessons we had wished didn't need to be discerned
Like growth for growth's sake is cancer's ideology
And we'd all be much better off with a lot more modesty

There is nothing uglier than hate and intimidation
A climate created by a noisy few insisting on damnation
That needed to be the fumble into life's brutality
When we might choose to fight instead for morality

That comes from fighting a crooked sort of government
To bring back and make simplicity something permanent
Weirdly, though, life only teaches impermanence and death
As we fight the system until the groan of our last breath

It is patriotic to fight the system that hurts us all
We've learned that present society is a stew to be recalled
Because it's led by the floating scum risen to the murky top
It's become patriotic to fight a government that will not stop

Like the Only Bible Read
by Michael Doyle

Let's live lives like the only Bible read
Walking witnesses of Jesus raised from the dead
Easter and Christmas hold nothing over immersion
Our faithful testimony given in baptism

It symbolizes our public proclamation
And is not a simple act of association
This then sets the core of our foundation
Moving us forward while also acting in denunciation

Of our old selves, emerging into the new
With promises to Jesus and ourselves as we renew
Purging ourselves of our old sinful ways
To walk with found faith into our new days

Truth be told, it's the ultimate act of individual choice
Choosing how we'll live and speaking it with our own voice
Learning to live from God's love from the beginning
And turn a losing hand played out into true living

Tailor fit: there is nothing in us that escapes detection
As God loves us in our every ounce of perfected imperfection
The fullness of us is open to His revealing examination
Yet still, the story, our stories, is one of His fascination

In our view, baptism might be seen as if like a wedding ring
Stating our promise publicly with all that we bring
That the Bible is the center-cut diamond, shining bright
In it, Romans explains the law revealed as being right

God's grace is sufficient for our soul's blessed security
We know that our salvation is for all of heavenly eternity
And the world we walk in our steps closest to Hell
We will know, with our salvation, it is in Heaven we will dwell

Like all sinners caught in our errors, yet remaining proud
We live our lives in repentance as forgiveness is allowed
None of us walk without knowing we need to improve our caliber
Yet, knowing that Jesus is waiting to develop our character

Conversion comes first with God's love, and then we love others
Learning to walk in accord with Heaven's love for one another
God loves us enough to transform us through the Holy Spirit
If only we are truly willing to obey as we lovingly hear it

We struggle and sometimes find we come up short or wrong
We know we are justified in His holy name, and that we belong
Truly living in Christ, as our living shield and salvation
Our truth and purpose are found in living out our translation

Whatever troubles may come our way, there can be no disputation
That nothing that comes our way will bring our separation
Given our lives' treasured spaces, there are no lasting traces
That can take us from God's loving and redemptive embraces

The Truth of Dust Roads Taken
by Michael Doyle

Some of the deepest truths are told in fiction,
Especially those of times of historical friction.
Pushed into competition over narrowed resources,
Inherent conflicts rise as nature takes its course.

Some conflicts come with visible tags of shame,
Where pointed fingers hold ghosts to their blame.
It is there in this vivid, haunting darkness
That the human race feels its way out of harshness.

An author chooses the moment to grow a tale told,
Looking forward or looking back, to praise or scold.
This is exceptionally true for the Dust Bowl of the Depression
And the immensity of its lasting impression.

It was a time when we learned just what people will do.
In hard times, sin disappears, and there is little virtue.
Strength grows in learning how it is to barely survive.
And tenacity is found in struggling to stay alive.

It was a time of failure leading to desperation and wrath
And a straightforward time with an easier sort of math.
Adding up to learning to live without certainty in life,
Wishing for some semblance of peace in the middle of strife.

All this type of desperation only leads to deeper thoughts
Like the sort of truths we should have always sought.
The rot of lives ruined is a putrid drip into the earth,
Destroyed by the ignorance and greed of man brings the dearth

That deprives humanity of the tears that cannot be realized,
As the sorrow burned deep beyond our souls death symbolized.
This is the heavy vintage that cannot age well through the ages.
Humanity's final death prophesized on our own tainted pages.

Time and Illusion

by Michael Doyle

Walking through life's many miles,
I count my wins with my smiles.
Some might think I've been abused.
But mostly, I stand amused.

All the countless false charges,
Are designed by enemies to somehow enlarge,
The bad things I've sometimes done.
In the end, I think it's me who has won.

Laid across my feathery bed,
Whispering traces through my head,
All this time and it's illusions
Have walked me past any confusion.

Fighting the clock of future recollections,
Laughing at the points in their connections,
I'm no longer nostalgic about my sorrow.
Instead, I lean in hard for my tomorrow.

I have seen that you're as big as you love,
Guided there when I listen to God above.
And that you're as small as what annoys
You into irritation above all of life's joys.

When we allow lesser evils to open our doors,
The greater evils find their way to pour
Through and compete with better opportunities.
It seems so subtle how we lose to the impurity.

Conversely, we find friendship multiplies the good,
While dividing all the evil that is understood.
Finding good advice in the humorous jokes we tell,
The smile shared is deeper than the best details.

In the end, we find we are not prisoners behind
The locked doors of the ignorance of closed minds,
Especially when we read what others will not read
And, in this, begin to find the clarity that we need.

"And this is his commandment,
that we believe in the
name of his Son Jesus
Christ and love one another,
just as he has commanded
us. Whoever keeps his
commandments abides in
God, and God in him"

1 John 3:23-24

Examining the Gifts of Love
by Michael Doyle

God's love brings tears to our eyes
Opened wide, we look, and we recognize
That all we live comes from God's love
As we keep our hearts fixed on God above

Agape love is the primary emphasis
That takes us through life's tempests
With God healing us fully and completely
This is the love that completes you and me

God's love is redemptive in its healing
Despite the temptations of free will reeling
God, the Father, asks us to be His reflection
It's in right understanding that we find direction

The love verse is written for us all
We are wise when, in gratitude, we recall
The paths and means of doing this right
These are the ways that precious in His sight

Corinth was a point of necessary convergence
As such, it was a place of proven influence
A center point that fought the establishment
Of Christ's church as something permanent

All brothers and sisters should come to agree
Healing divisions while keeping sight on destiny
We are all followers of Christ as one body
We should keep that straight and reflect boldly

Preferences take seed subject to Godly correction
Leadership and lordship must set the direction
Setting our eyes on God and Jesus in Heaven above
The level ground of purpose is set in His love

Do we speak with love or be a resounding gong?
It is the love we need that allows us to belong
Rejoicing with truth, protective in every way
Putting away childlike ways to perfect our living days

Faith, hope, and love get us to our destination
With love being the greatest truth, without hesitation
For all the gifts are important but come from love
And this love brings us the fruits from above

Love holds more wonder than the miracles we live
It is the primary drive behind all that we give
This is the importance of living out Christ's virtue
Because loving others is what is right and true

Accepting healing or atonement is soul revealing
Moving so much further than simply feeling
Salvation brings the healing that is truly needed
This is the point that must be heeded

Every good thing comes from above
God's thumbprint of approval is for those who love
This is that path away from deprivations of the soul
Learning to be servants of love is our true roles

The chasm of my soul craves earnestly for God above
Let me walk in this light and learn to truly love
It is love that drives out the world's darkness
And removes the lens that brings a life of harshness

I pray this to come for all in the pending week
That love be the answer that openly speak
Guiding us to be gentle and in all ways kind
Keeping God's love in all ways and always on our minds

Sweet Victory
by Michael Doyle

Nothing can take God's place.
I've felt His glory, face-to-face.
I am grateful from my heart.
He's been here from the start.

Saving me from my transgressions
And from all this world's aggressions.
It's amazing all that He's done,
In the trinity of Father, Holy Spirit, and Son.

From my badness, He has brought good,
From my madness, something understood.
I see it in the faces of my daughters
Of whom He has blessed me as their father.

There is happiness in my attitude.
Thanks to the blessings, I know gratitude.
He's given me my full restoration
Through the path of my healing redemption.

His love reigns over my eternity,
I live forevermore convinced of His deity.
With His voice silencing my enemies,
His is the path to reaching my sweet victory.

Anchored In Grace

by Michael Doyle

We stand as ambassadors,
In this world of brokenness,
Presenting loving truth,
Yet, sometimes noted for outspokenness.

All that we possess has been given
By our God who is truly living.
Our response is one of contemplation.
It leads to our redemption.

Its fullness is our life's story.
It becomes a study of true glory.
We believe the Gospel is an open door.
It brings the life of blessings we have in store.

God is omnipotent even as he gives us His love.
To our blessing, it fits snugly as a glove.
God is fully aware of our all too human faces,
Still, He is there to lovingly give us grace.

It is through God's will and not our own
That we come before His heavenly throne.
We know that God remains the same in every way
As you and I go through a process, day-to-day.

Anchored in grace, we know our way.
In knowing this, we know what to do and say
As we model Jesus in all that we do.
To our best, we are the children of God and true.

This knowledge is borne with fascination.
Within this truth, we find our motivation.
Step by step, we walk toward our maturity
Until we dutifully serve the blessed doxology.

No retreat; no surrender, and no sort of regret,
Ours is to live a life we're not meant to forget.
Charging on to the benefit of our God's glory,
This is our minor part in His greater story.

Heaven's Hope

by Michael Doyle

Heaven's hope is forever
So maybe it's clever
That we listen when angels cry
With our hands lifted to the sky.

We proclaim our love in Jesus's name,
Doing our best to remove all blame.
We speak the truth of our claim
That by God's grace, we're freed from shame.

Putting on the grace of rightful attitude,
Our faith and belief move beyond platitude.
Into the actions brought by our dedication,
Knowing and serving God's will is our motivation.

Angels and believers join together to sing.
Together we worship the holiness of our king,
Knowing that it's in Him we find our worth,
We keep our eyes on our true North.

Singing together, our voices join as one.
We honor the glory of our Father and the Son.
Thankful, we praise the Lord on high
With our hands raised toward the sky.

Concerns for Perennial Truths

by Michael Doyle

Admittedly, I grew up differently,
Believing in my nation and God reverently.
Strength of character and in spirit,
Where the battle was righteous, I would bear it.

I have watched as our ideals were beaten down,
And somehow Marxism claimed society's crown.
But now I stand a little prouder and see the possibility
Of rising above the din and its mass anxiety.

I see a nation on the brink of its discovery
That it can stand for righteousness in its recovery.
It's a return to the permanent things that bring prosperity,
And it begins by understanding our nation's sovereignty.

Moral order, self-government, and having a national purpose
Are the fundamentals by which we understand our service.
There will be no clinging to the burning embers of technocracy.
The people will remember our truths and return to dignity.

For most of my life, I have seen our self-confidence decline,
Wondering to myself whatever happened to this republic of mine.
Self-expression was freedom, not self-control and responsibility.
Self-governance was no longer believed within our capability.

The market didn't raise the children; neither did the latchkey.
The economy hollowed out as we rediscovered the need for family.
Yet, the elites tell us knowing biology is hardened bigotry.
We will not sacrifice on the altar of convenience and identity.

Our republic requires the People's moral formation.
Fundamental truths are not a matter of anyone's imagination.
We refuse conformance to any taxing demands of globalism
On the conviction that meaning is what brings optimism.

An old adage states that it is always darkest before the dawn,
But it's by the dawn's early light that we now make our move on
Ridding ourselves of the decrepit ways of foul-minded liberalism
The bureaucracy will be replaced by our renewed conservatism.

We are rebuilding the American Republic for every Main Street
While putting aside any feigned alliance with any Wall Street
That fails to understand the necessity of our own sovereignty.
It is the only means to dream and restore our nation's dignity.

There is no need or purpose in apologizing for civilization.
Instead, we must live ours for the greatness of this nation.
The economy and our global friendships exist for our family
Not the other way around as we begin to restore our dignity.

Faithful in Time and Grace

by Michael Doyle

I'd be the one mistaken
If I didn't notice when I was shaken,
And that God provides my foundation
When I build my life in my station.

As a believer in my confession,
There is no struggle without conditions.
There is no way I'll fail
When I know that God always prevails.

Faithful in time and grace,
Through God's love, I know my place.
Reminded daily of all that I've been given,
I know that I'm blessed and forgiven.

Though the rains may torrentially fall,
All that I have to do is call
His holy name and it gets me through
Whatever this world might happen to do.

There's so much to hold in contemplation,
As I think about my blessed redemption.
Calling on the Lord's holy name,
He has given me blessings that cover my shame.

Soul Rot

by Michael Doyle

When your bad is so good
That it's become understood
As being what you're best at,
It may be best to remember that.

It's not exactly forgot.
You're suffering from soul rot.
Staring death in the face,
And keeping it in its place.

You keep on constantly bleeding,
Not knowing what you're needing.
And the doctors really can't help you now
As you keep muddling through somehow.

Proud that you've kept on your feet
In the face of yet another bloody defeat.
You'll fight on to the bitter end
Even as the Reaper becomes your only friend.

It's a burning sort of feeling,
A fire that keeps your head reeling.
Screaming to yourself as you piss blood,
You pull yourself through crawling the mud.

Given the soul-searching choice,
You look hard to find your truest voice.
I'd rather be a heart than a brain,
But wouldn't that just be in vain?

Because, you see I simply forgot
That I have a chronic case of soul rot.
Does it come across as shaded,
If my interest in life has faded?

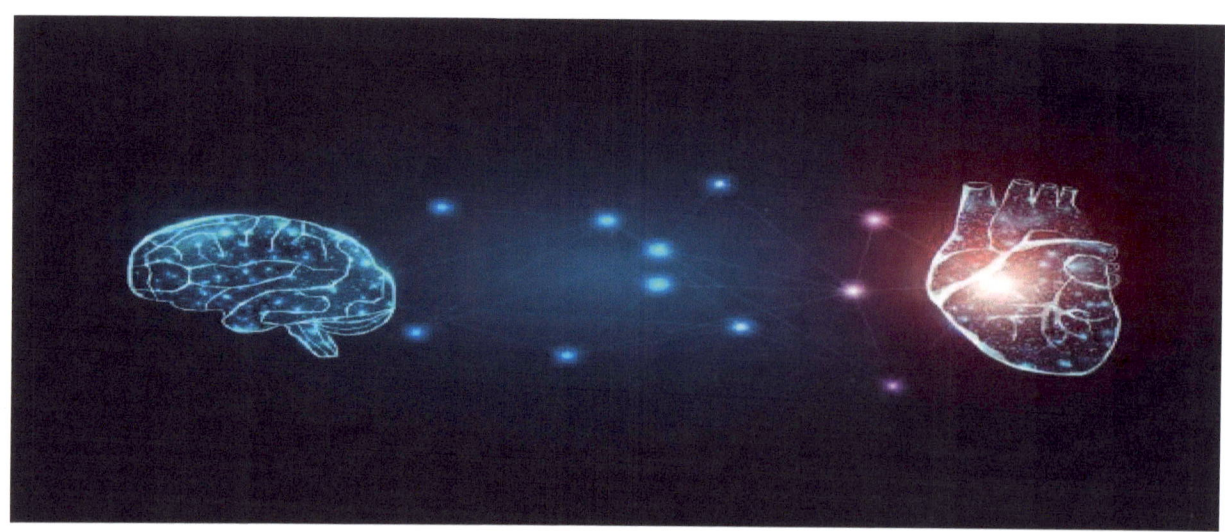

Serving as the Lord Serves Us

by Michael Doyle

God's wrath is at Satan's snare;
Seeking to keep evil at bay and fair.
The path forward for humanity
Is best walked with modest humility.

Across the level ground under the cross,
We keep aware of Christ's loss.
In doing as He did, He gave us salvation,
Ensuring us our heavenly destination.

Building mankind's bridge with mystery,

It's simply a matter of theological history.
First, the Jews, then, the Gentiles received an open-door
So that the world might live for a little more.

Our rebellious nature draws us apart and keeps us down,
Until we repent and grow into the victor's crown.
A remnant remains willing to receive God's love,
It is this acceptance that brings us to Heaven above.

So often, we get it wrong and God makes it right,
Removing the darkest traces by His holy light.
His winds sail us across Jesus's beautiful sea,
Bringing us to the harbor of His sweet victory.

Those who live under Christ are blessed beyond measure,
Knowing holiness as our best and greatest treasure.
The roots of God support the branch3es of humanity,
Nourishing us as we serve Him in our humility.

It is God who provides us with His providence.
By His grace, it is ours to receive His abundance.
It is God's good ability that gives us the capability
To move beyond our earthbound infirmities.

Each day we wake up to new sets of opportunities,
We need only look out for all that we might be.
These are the gifts from God by which we serve,
And become His ambassadors the world deserves.

It is ours to seek out their rightful application,
And to serve ceaselessly in our faithful dedication.
Giving to the world as God has made us each malleable,
We are to live love as best that we are capable.

We live in a world of brokenness
Forging our words of praise in our outspokenness.
We must each do our best to serve as examples
Of what God's love is and demonstrate it as being ample.

We are not better than, but instead, better for.
Always inviting others to know God's love is pure.
Not acting in blatant ignorance or living in pride,
But keeping mindful of the living God inside.

Works of righteousness come from God alone
If we boast pridefully, we'll need to atone.
Ego is known to edge God out and is not the way.
God encourages us to walk humbly in this way.

A head full of knowledge without a heart's love
Unwittingly detracts others' eyes from Heaven above.
In all that we do, we need to learn to walk humbly,
Setting into God's example, and doing so gently.

Echoing the Grace

by Michael Doyle

Worthy of the Lord's call,
I am prayerful about all.
I feel His joy everyday
As He changes my every way.

The Holy Spirit guides me,
Overflowing inside of me.
There is a need for His strength
As long as the day's length.

My holy king is worthy of praise.
In His power, He will raise
A choir of angels to sing,
Echoing the grace that He brings.

Hearts healed are what is found.
Bodies are made whole and it's profound.
I hear the Lord's voice ring out,
And I am thankful that He removes my doubt.

I know who my heart belongs to,
The Son of God is phenomenally true.
This time is one as is every blessed hour.
I will remain guided by His love and power.

A Holy Genealogy
by Michael Doyle

It didn't really begin with the rolling back of a stone
As Jesus reached out to prove we are not alone.
The church was born to spread the faith of our gospel
Allowing believers to have assurance that all is well.

In our acceptance and then our believing,
We came to find an endless stream of our receiving
The very goodness of God that we need.
It's there on the Bible's pages to read.

The good news given is addressed to be known by all
Among every walk that answers faithfully to God's call.
From the beginning, our has openly said
The gospel belongs to all to whom their souls are not dead.

All who are chosen, are chosen by grace.
It doesn't matter about works in this kind of race.
Hope is the blessed treasure and its loving discovery
Is the beginning and end of each soul's recovery.

Whispered tenderly for our earnest contemplation
Is God's holy play for humanity's redemption.
Examining the chronological history shows no deviation,
But transparently offered for our open inspection.

To understand, you need to know Jewish History,
If we are to know and understand our theology.
God's redemptive plan has been God's pattern
Moving man toward good and away from our sin.

Our deepest struggles are as close as our souls.
Despite this truth, God has given us self-control.
From faithfully living as God tells us to do,
We will discern and live what is holy, good, and true.

This is a great banquet we should not decline,
Whatever the infirmity, it is for all to dine.
There is always room with God's open door
To bring in the hurting and faithful for more.

God brings love and healing under His grace.
We need only to accept God with our full embrace.
Our story rises up from the purity of history
To make a holy remnant into His holy family.

The wisest words that come to our wounded hearts
Can be traced back to the very start.
Christ died for our sins that we might live
God given atonement allows Him to forgive.

Believing in Blessings

by Michael Doyle

Encountering the profound,
I praise the goodness I have found.
Looking into God's face,
I find myself touched by His grace.

I have nothing left to prove,
Loving to watch God as He moves
The world with His ways.
I've seen a lot in my passing days.

What would it take to believe
All the blessings I receive?
Not just in my past,
But the best of all are those that last.

Making Jesus known in my praise
Of the Son, our Father has raised.
Given to us as our salvation,
I see His love spread across the nation.

I've encountered the profound.
Glory is what it is that I have found.
Loving life through God's loving trace,
I find myself touched by His Grace

Let Love Forever Echo

by Michael Doyle

Let love forever echo
Every moment's hello
Spoken by Jesus's name
Within the holy picture frame.

Life is known like a fire,
Filled with arguable desire.
To walk in His power,
Reborn with every passing hour.

He brings this joy we're feeling,
As I walk through my healing.
Bringing sight to the blind,
Knowing His love is the best we'll find.

Bringing light into the darkness,
Removing all essence of harshness.
Shining through the shadows,
His Love carries me everywhere I go.

Down to life's final wire,
His love burns like a holy fire.
There is peace in His presence,
Changing my life with its essence.

Coming to Faith

by Michael Doyle

Jesus is known by His many names.
These are revealed as we examine Biblical claims.
We find it is with prayerful consideration
That there is power in every faithful iteration.

In the shadow and light of His sacrifice and resurrection,
We live our faith life inside its connections.
Each makes us more blessed every passing day.
We learn to follow and live Christ in every way.

The Book of Romans gives a lot to live on.
In many ways, it is like a spiritual marathon.
It takes a lot from us while giving us more.
It's the believer's constitution, intense and pure.

In reading through, there's a lot to getting ourselves right,
To live with dignity within the revealing of God's light.
Eventually, every knee will bow, and every tongue will confess.
Perhaps, then, we must strive to always do our best.

In understanding the depths of depravity and our sins,
We find the beauty of God's surpassing love again.
Knowing the truth of where it is that we daily dwell,
And rest in God's assurance that all is and will be well.

As we walk out onto the theological leading edge,
Our zeal is one not solely based on knowledge.
It is based on faith that Christ fulfills the law
And our is to fervently respond to His holy call.

We keep the word of God faithfully near.
We hold our beliefs to be quite dear.
Confessing that the Lord is our only salvation.
God's sacrifice came as our only needed explanation.

Trusting in the Lord, we know no need for shame,
Jew and Gentile call on his Holy, blessed name.
Calling on his known names, we find our way to salvation.
It is the path for our faithful nation.

Believing and living the Word's message heard,
This is the truth of the Gospel observed.
Though, at times, this seems maybe overly demanding,
God will and does supply our path to understanding.

Too often, we find ourselves an obstinate people,
Despite generations of being raised in the Temple.
All this to get to the point where we can discern
What it is that we all must know and need to learn.

It is in this moment of rational conversion,
We find God waiting for us in our observation
That sometimes we backslide into our surrender,
And finally, I find God's love to be warm and tender.

The best messages come with callouses grown,
Showing the truth without fear as it is known.
Faith shines through in the moments we share,
Professing our belief as deeply as we dare.

Each Day Is A Gift

by Michael Doyle

Each day, it seems, is a gift received
From God above, or so it is believed
But there is no real proof to be given
So, a little doubt might yet be forgiven.

Prayer doesn't change God, just the man,
And from this, confidence is taken as it can.
Thanksgiving alongside rightminded supplication
Is the fruit of the spirit, right for this nation.

Answers to prayers come in three flavors to savor.
Each of them according to God's plan without favor.
Played out as words as trite as yes, no, and maybe
Sometimes, I fall apart as it continues to slay me.

Twice removed from the beliefs of only yesterday,
I often find myself alone and stumbling along the way
The past is as deep as the evening's passing shadow.
But my faith sometimes hangs out in the shallows.

I find myself fighting the good fight every day.
Wondering why it is that this is the only way,
And wondering what the value is in what we pray
When our Father knows every word that we might say.

Answers to prayers come in three flavors to savor.
Each of them according to God's plan without favor.
Played out as words as trite as yes, no, and maybe
Sometimes, I fall apart as it continues to slay me.

I have seen better people than me taken harshly down.
I have seen the wisest of men made to look the clown.
Where it is, how it is when it is from the very start,
I know with faith that it begins inside my broken heart.

In our attempts at prayer, we learn to patiently exhale,
While God's spirit sometimes smiles as we learn to inhale.
This is not effort but the way that is according to God's plan,
And, after all, I am not an angel, just an ordinary man.

Answers to prayers come in three flavors to savor.
Each of them according to God's plan without favor.
Played out as words as trite as yes, no, and maybe
Sometimes, I fall apart as it continues to slay me.

The Call Of a
SHEPHERD'S
Song

MICHAEL DOYLE HAS BEEN BLESSED WITH TRAVELING WORLDWIDE SINCE HE WAS NINE WEEKS OLD. HE WAS BORN IN SCOTLAND TO A US NAVY FAMILY AND LATER ENLISTED IN THE NAVY. THESE TRAVELS INTRODUCED HIM TO THE WORLD FIRSTHAND, BUT AS A LIFETIME LEARNER, HE ALSO LEARNED TO SEE THE WORLD THROUGH THE EYES OF OTHERS.

FROM A YOUNG AGE, HE REALIZED THAT HE LIKED LEARNING AND SHARING NEW THINGS THROUGH PHOTOGRAPHY AND WRITING. ONE FORM OF WRITING HE ENJOYS IS POETRY FOCUSED ON TRAVEL, FAITH, AND HUMAN CONNECTIONS. IN HIS POETRY, HE OFTEN INVOKES THE ROLE OF A STORYTELLER. MICHAEL HAS HIS BACHELOR OF SCIENCE IN COMMUNICATION, MAGNA CUM LAUDE, FROM PURDUE UNIVERSITY GLOBAL.

JOIN MICHAEL AND FOLLOW HIS CONTINUING JOURNEY ON WWW.ALOHAPROMISESFOREVER.COM HIS DEBUT BOOK OF POETRY IS DEDICATED TO JESUS BECAUSE, AFTER ALL, GOD IS THE GREATEST CREATOR, AND THE BIBLE IS THE MOST EXTRAORDINARY TALE TOLD AND SHARED WITH HUMANITY. THE CALL OF A SHEPHERD'S SONG IS A DEEPLY PERSONAL AND SPIRITUAL JOURNEY EXPRESSED THROUGH POETRY THAT EXPLORES FAITH, GRACE, HUMILITY, AND THE QUIET BEAUTY FOUND IN LIFE'S SACRED MOMENTS. THROUGH HEARTFELT VERSES, READERS ARE INVITED TO REFLECT ON THE MEANING OF CHRISTMAS, THE STRENGTH FOUND IN SURRENDER, THE COMFORT OF PRAYER, AND THE QUIET COURAGE REQUIRED TO WALK IN TRUTH. EACH POEM IS A WHISPER OF ENCOURAGEMENT, A TESTAMENT TO GOD'S ENDURING LOVE, AND A REMINDER THAT WE ARE NEVER TRULY ALONE ON THIS PATH.